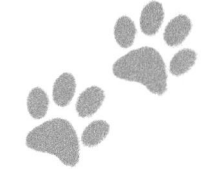

# My Little Big Cats Coloring Book

## This Book Belongs To:

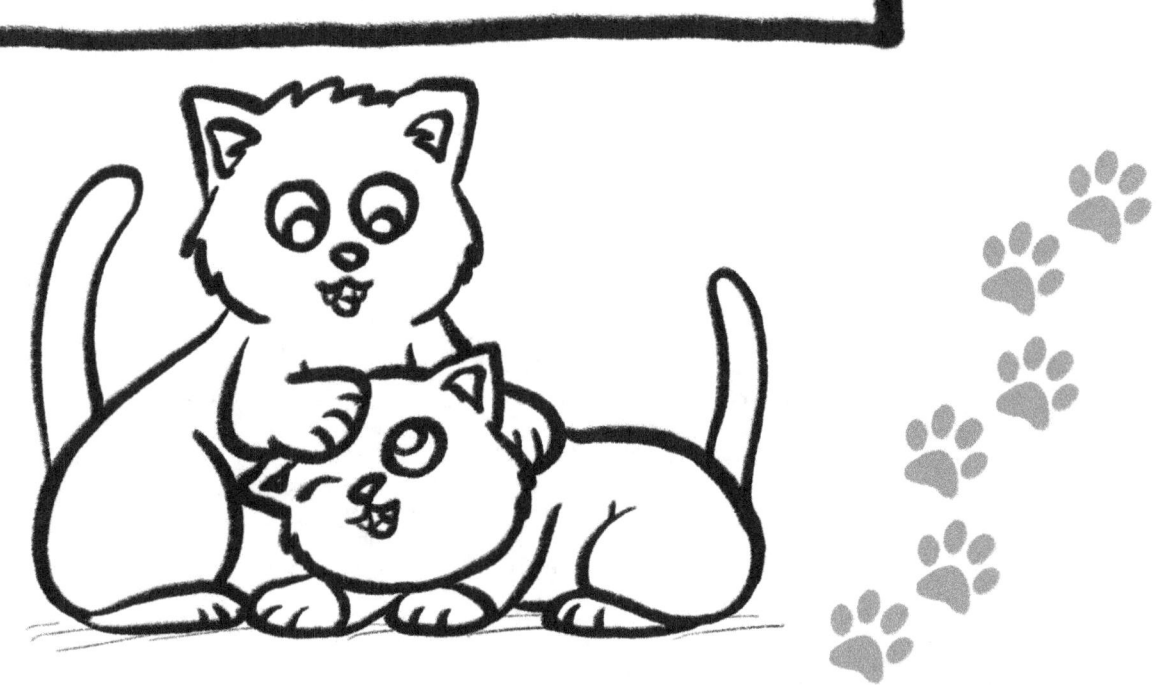

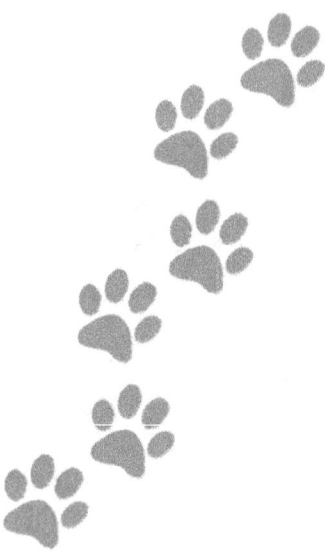

Little Big Coloring Books
My Little Big Cats Coloring Book
Copyright © 2024 by Morten Nygaard Pedersen
All rights reserved. No part of this publication may be reproduced, distributed, or transmitted in any form or by any means, including photocopying, recording, or other electronic or mechanical methods, without the prior written permission of the publisher, except in the case of brief quotations embodied in critical reviews and certain other noncommercial uses permitted by copyright law.
For information, address playfulhousepublishing@gmail.com
Little Big Books
Playful House Publishing
www.playfulhousepublishing.com

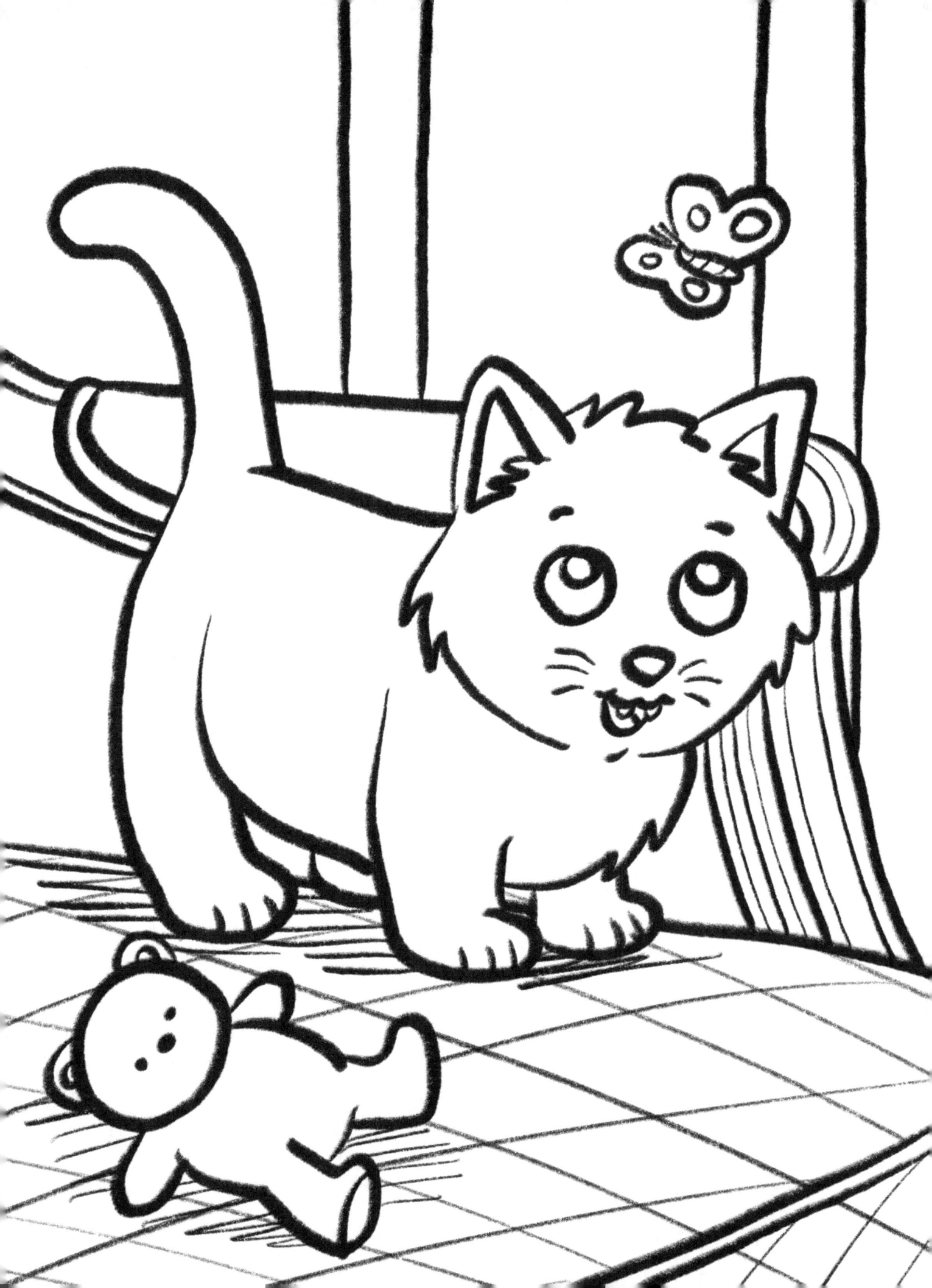

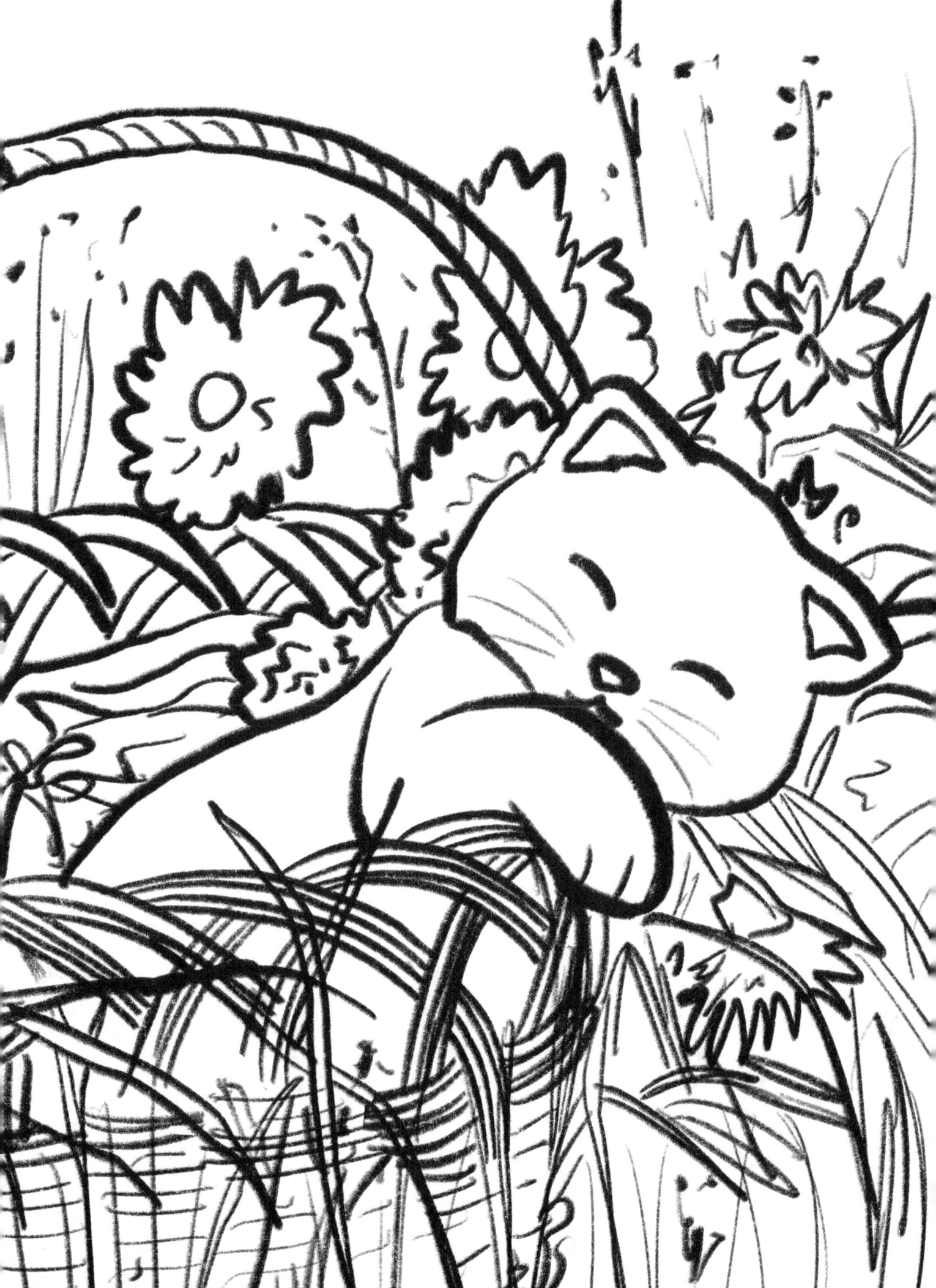

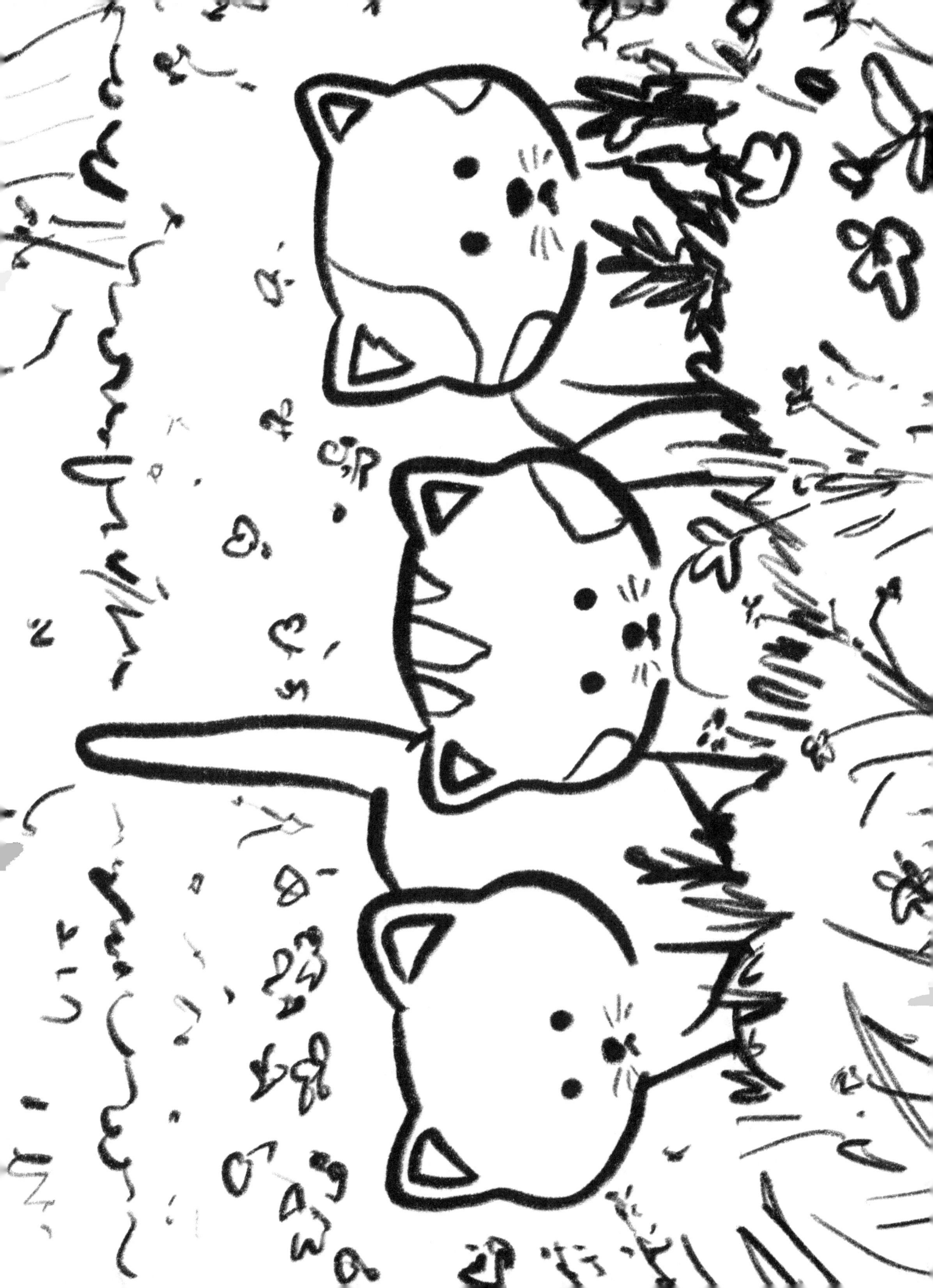

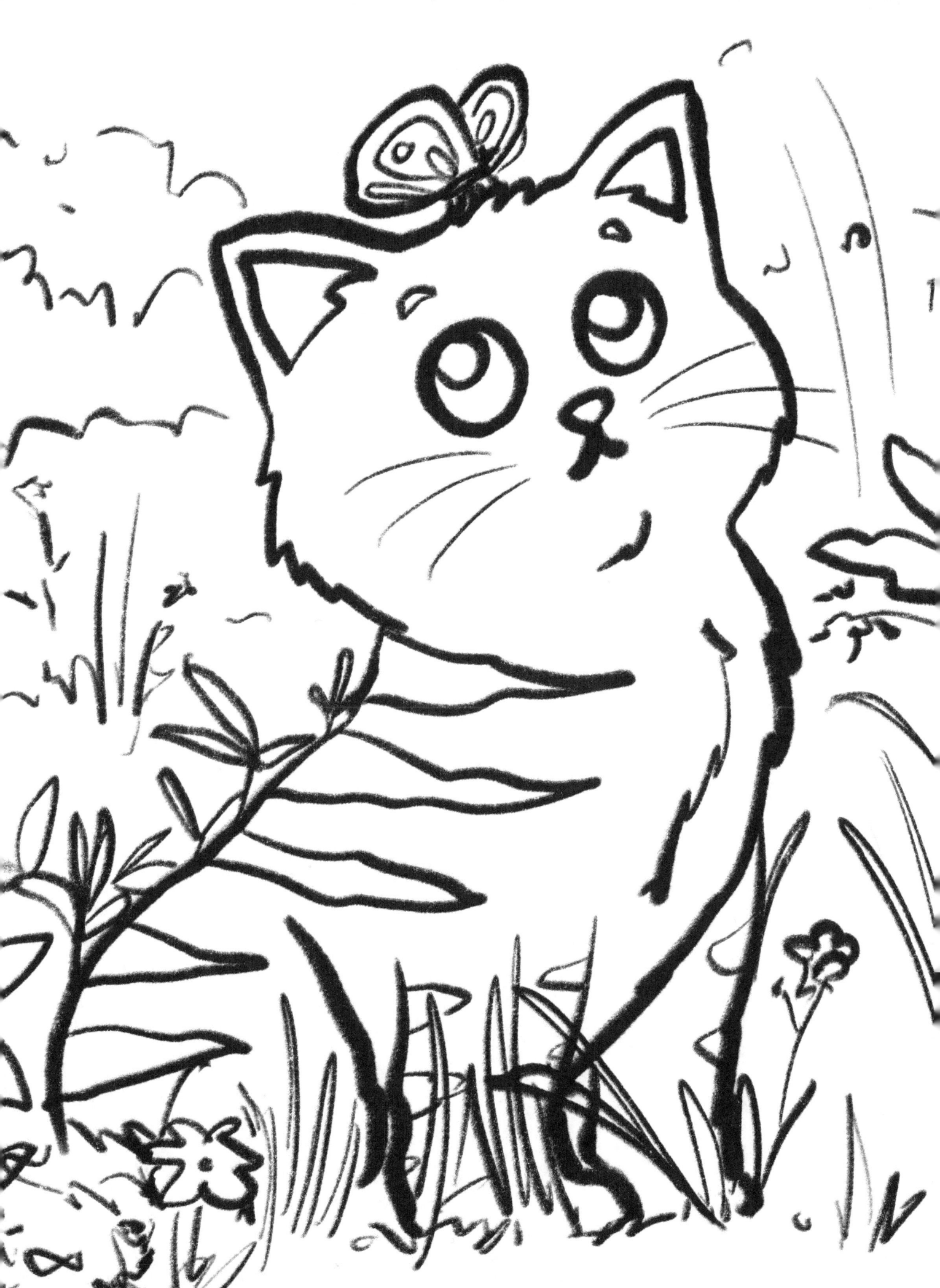

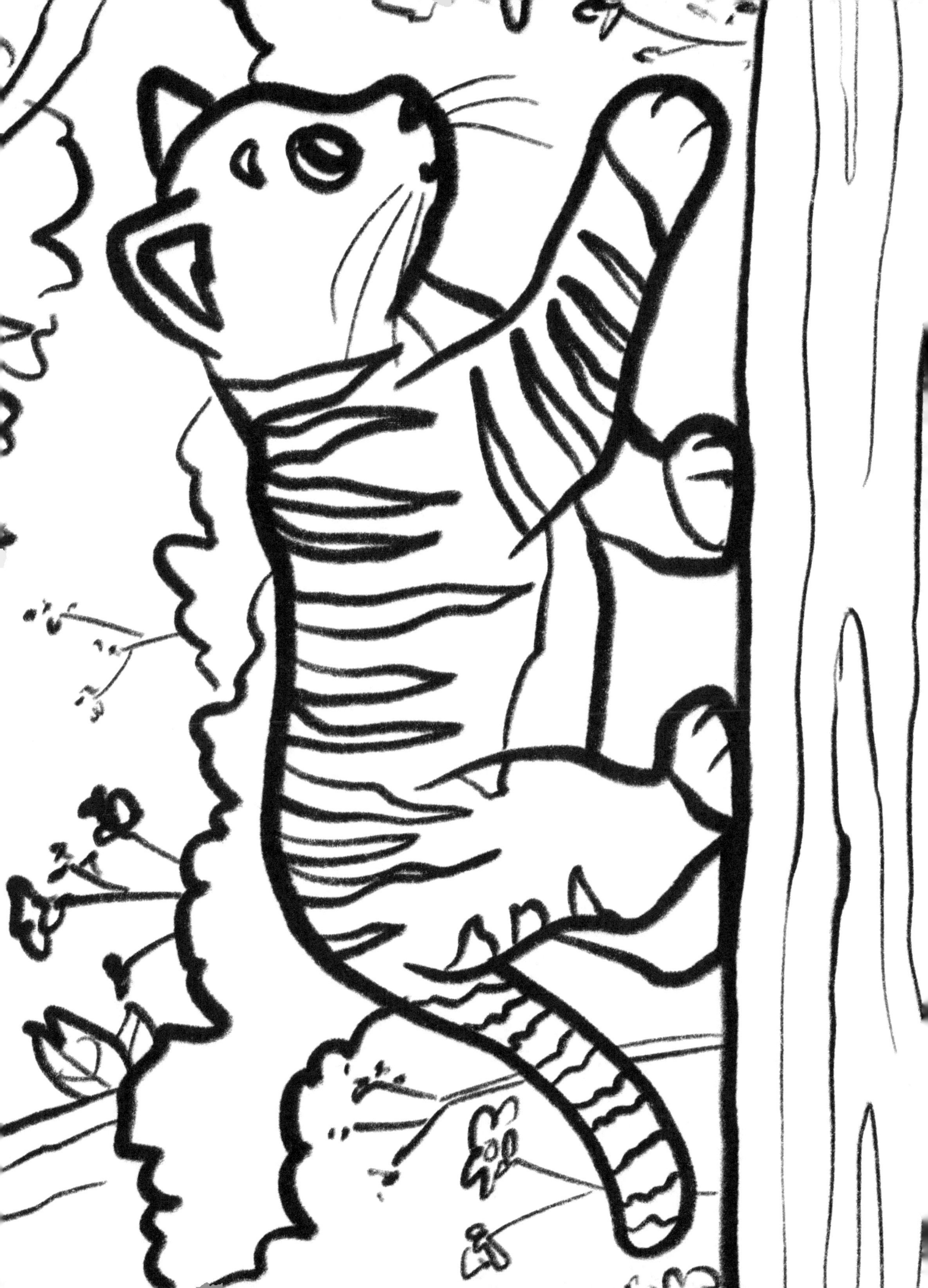

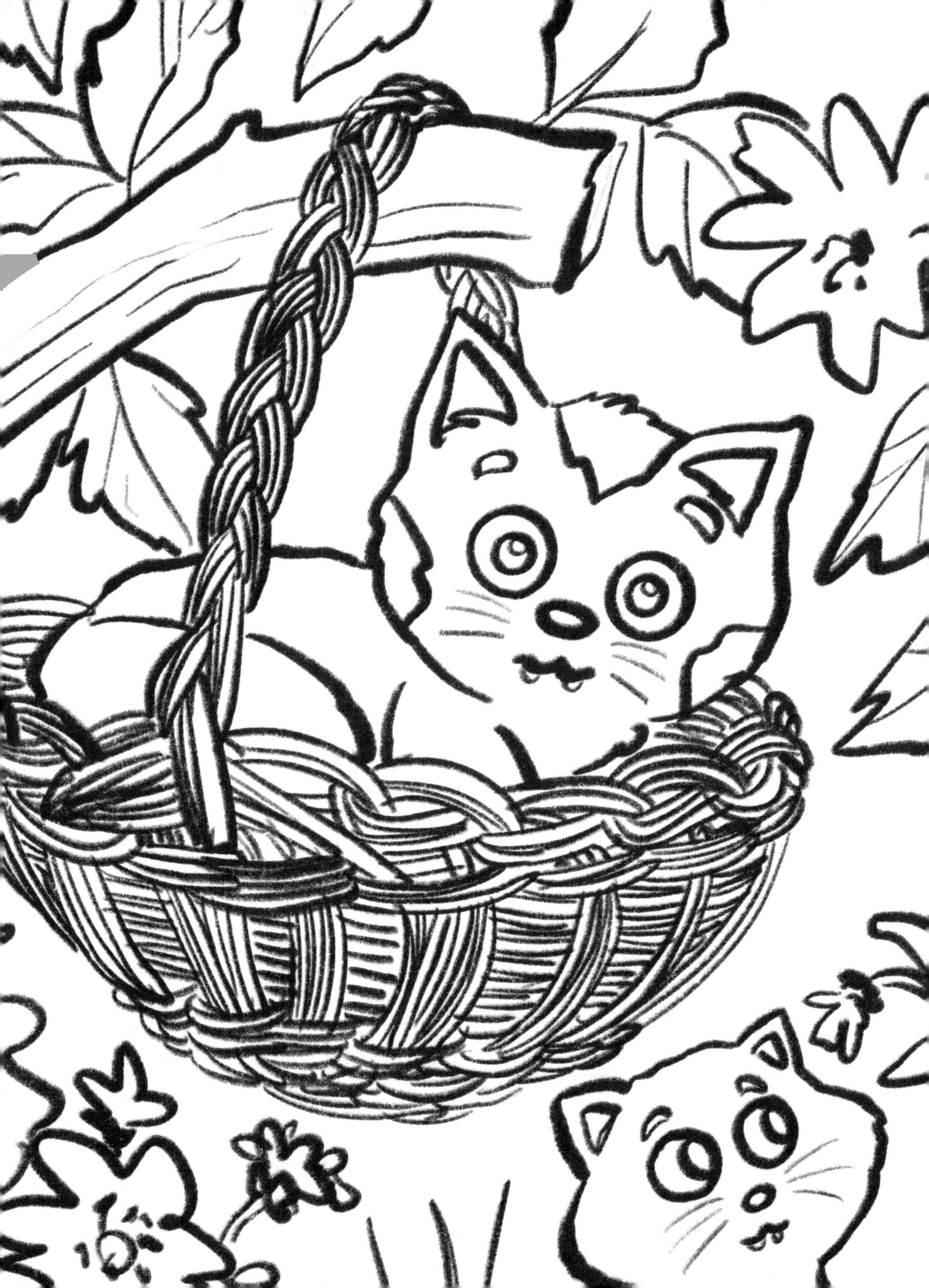

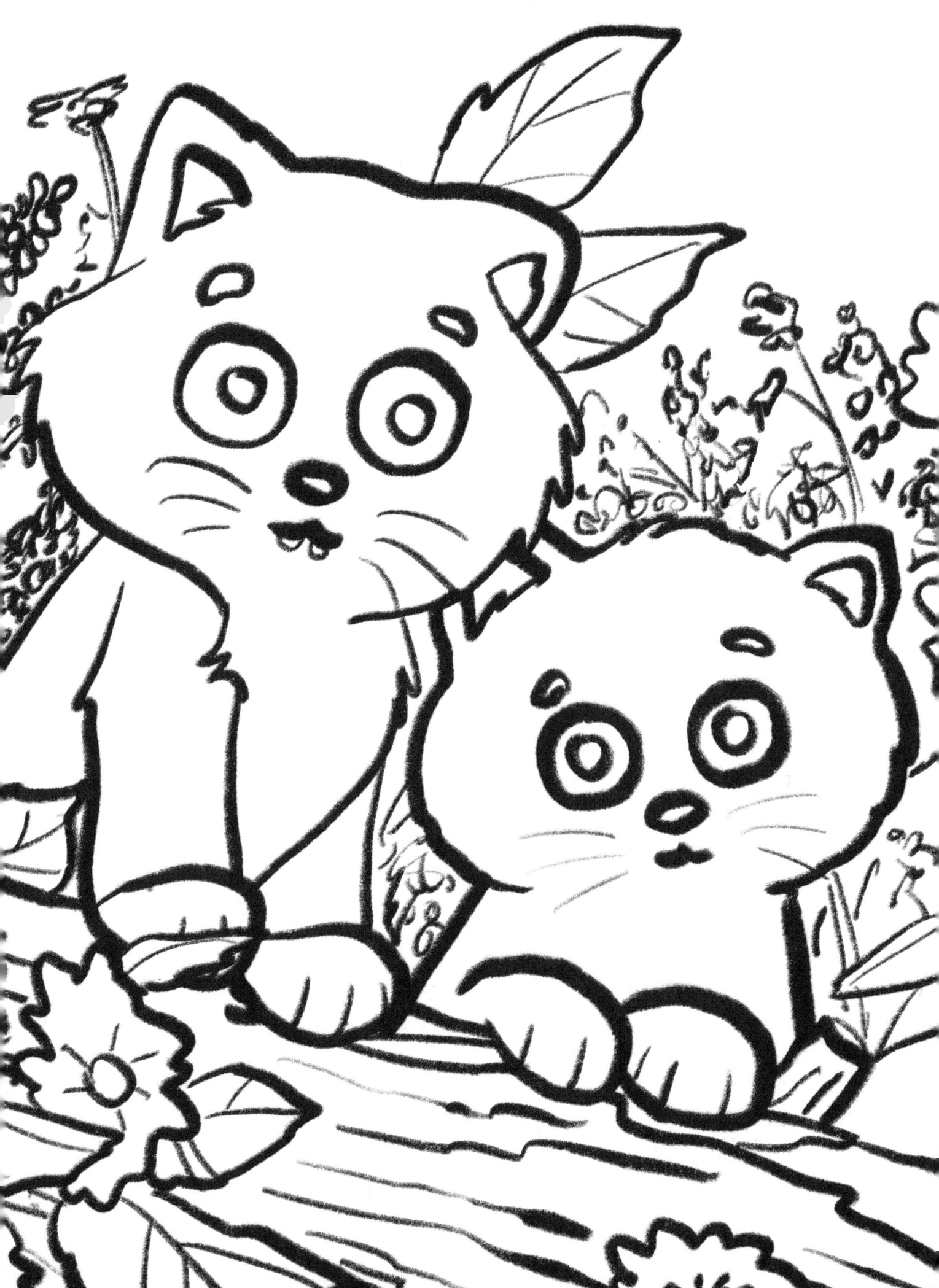

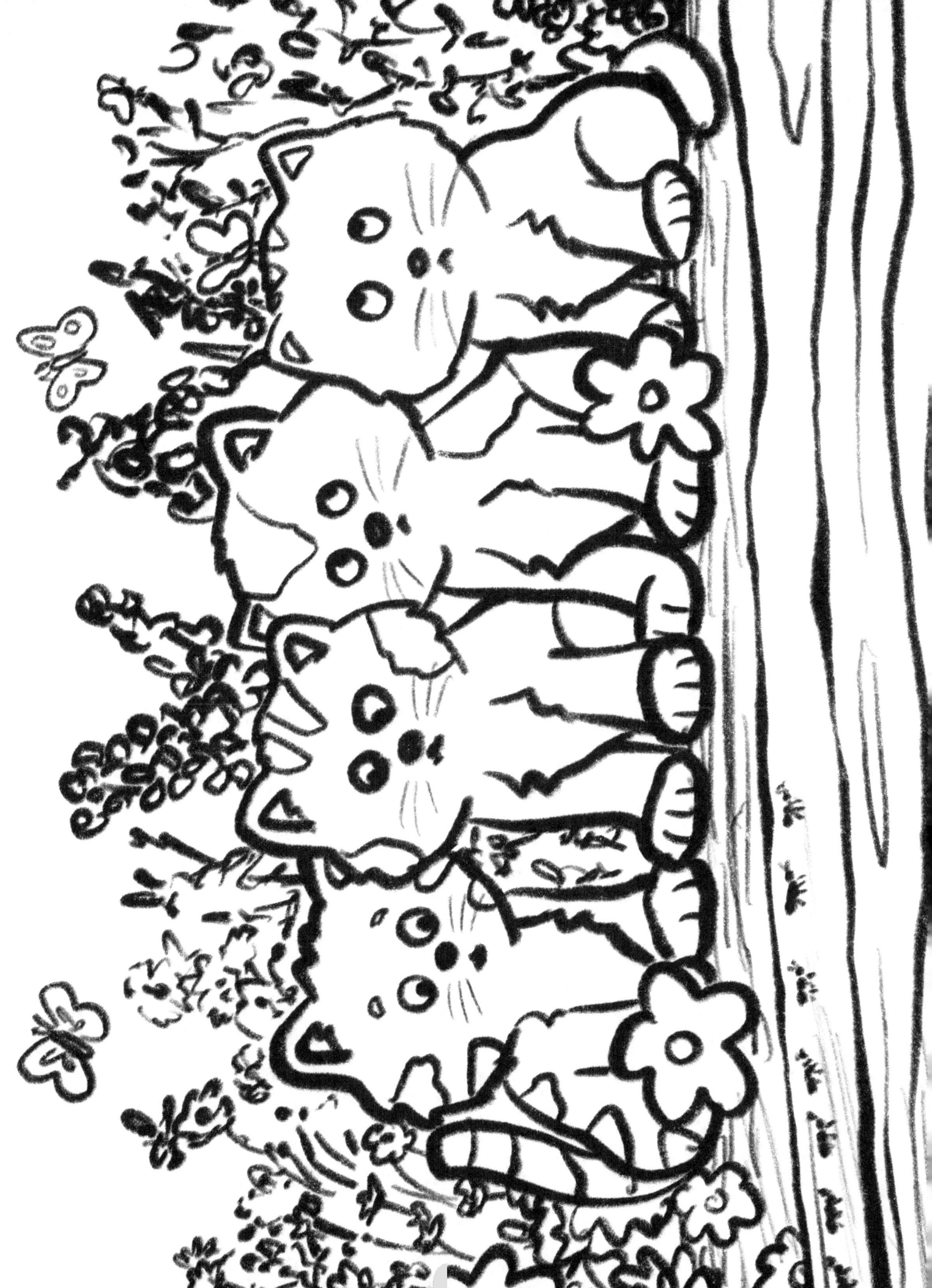

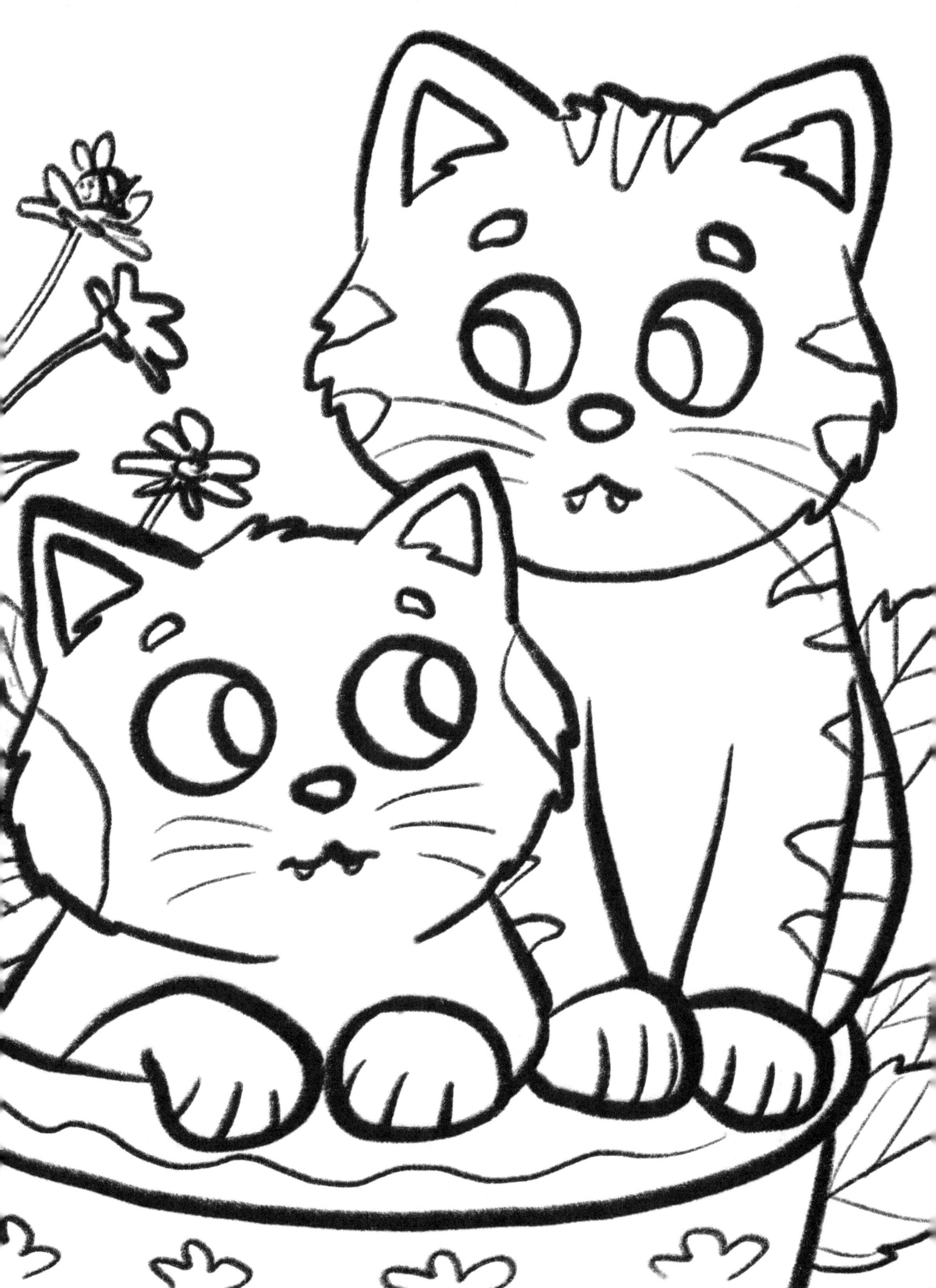

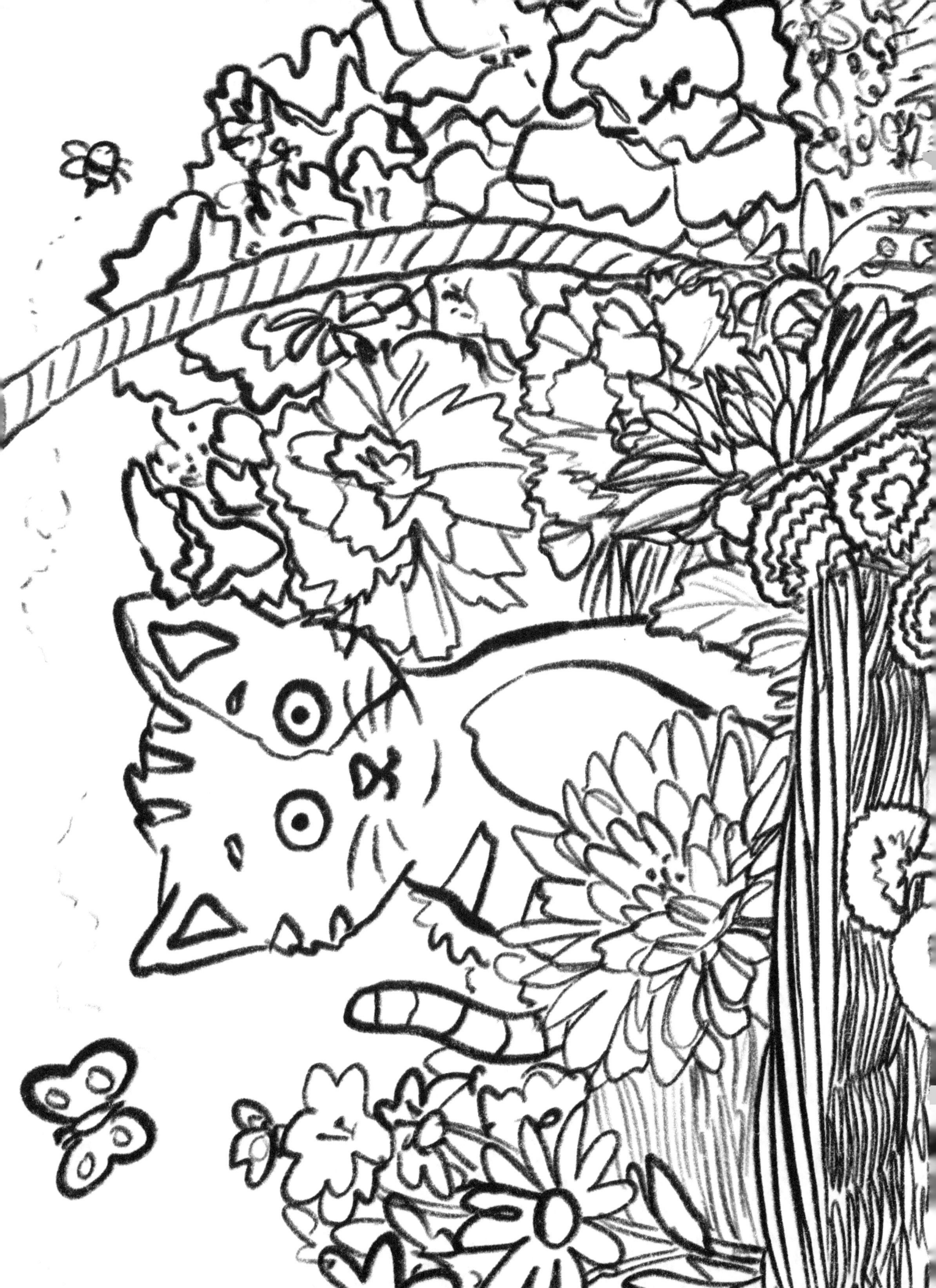

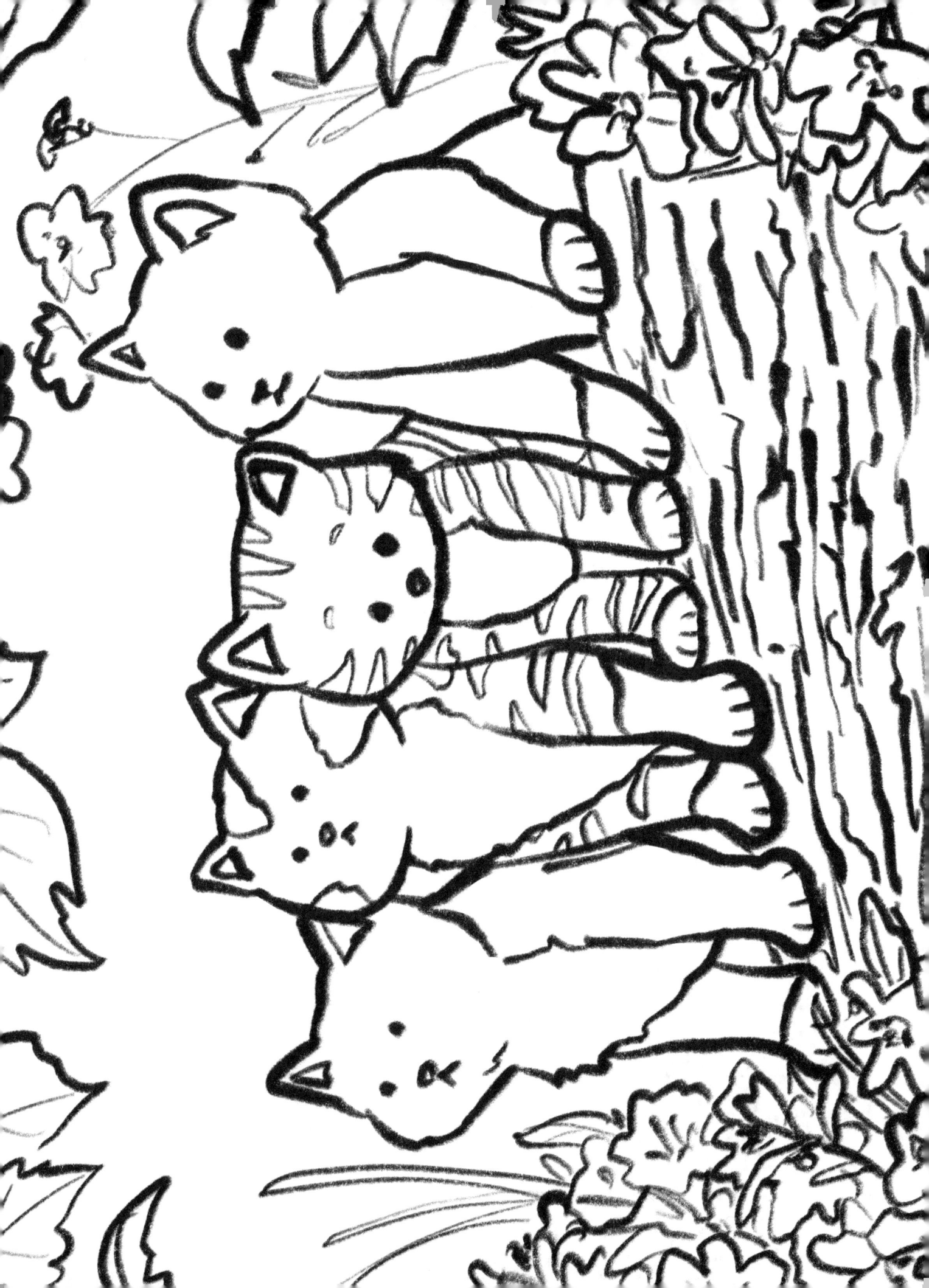

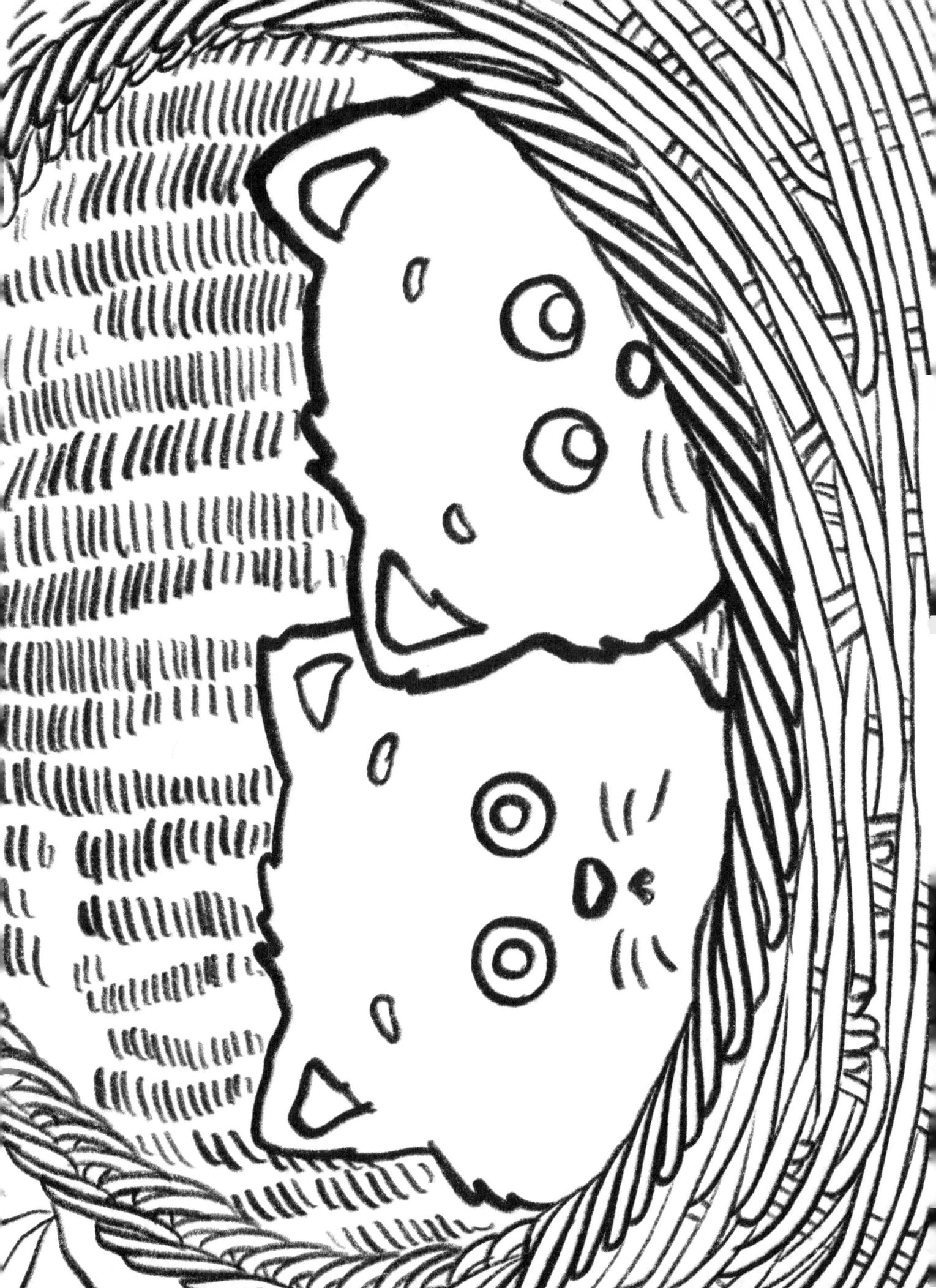

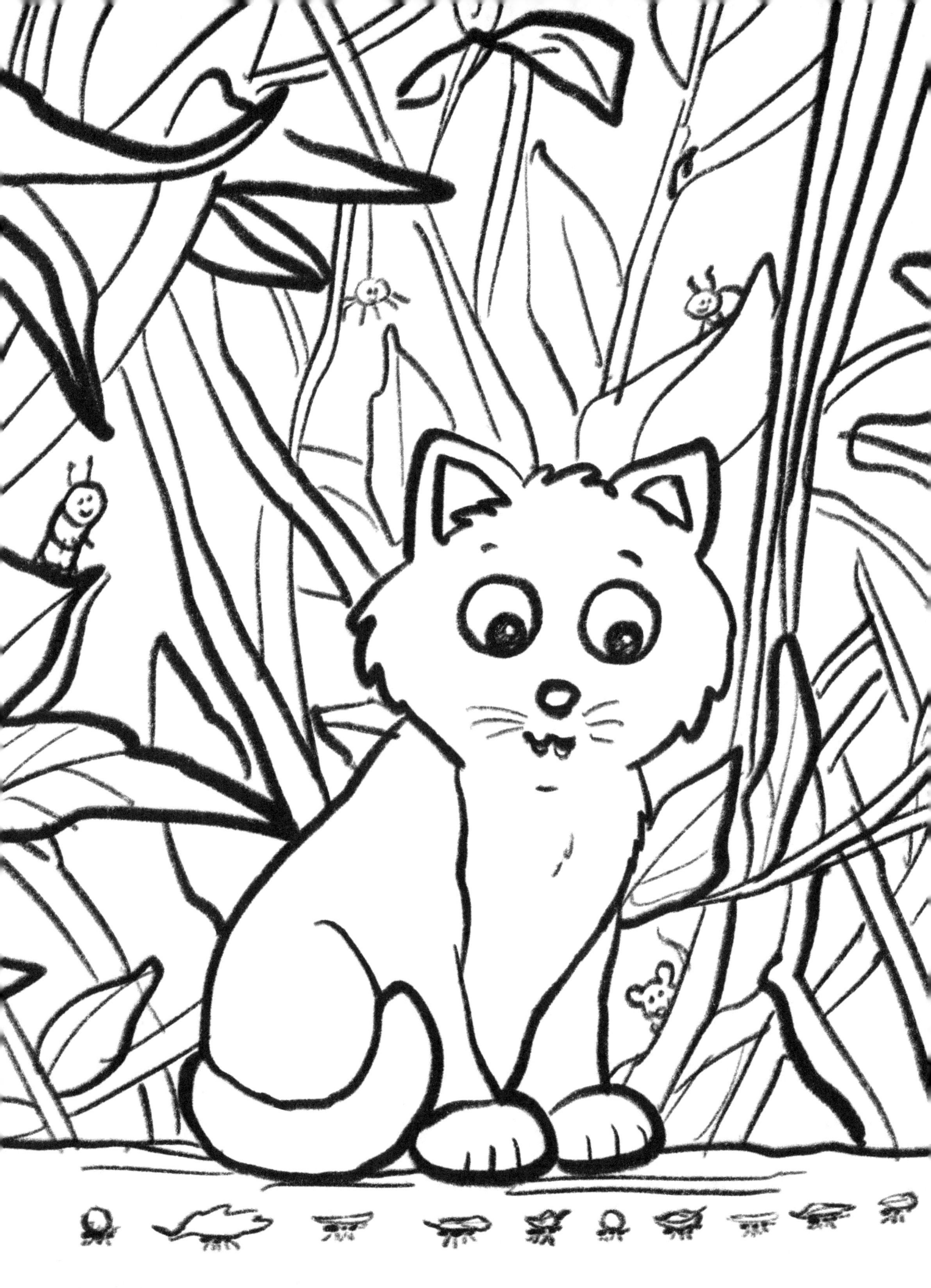

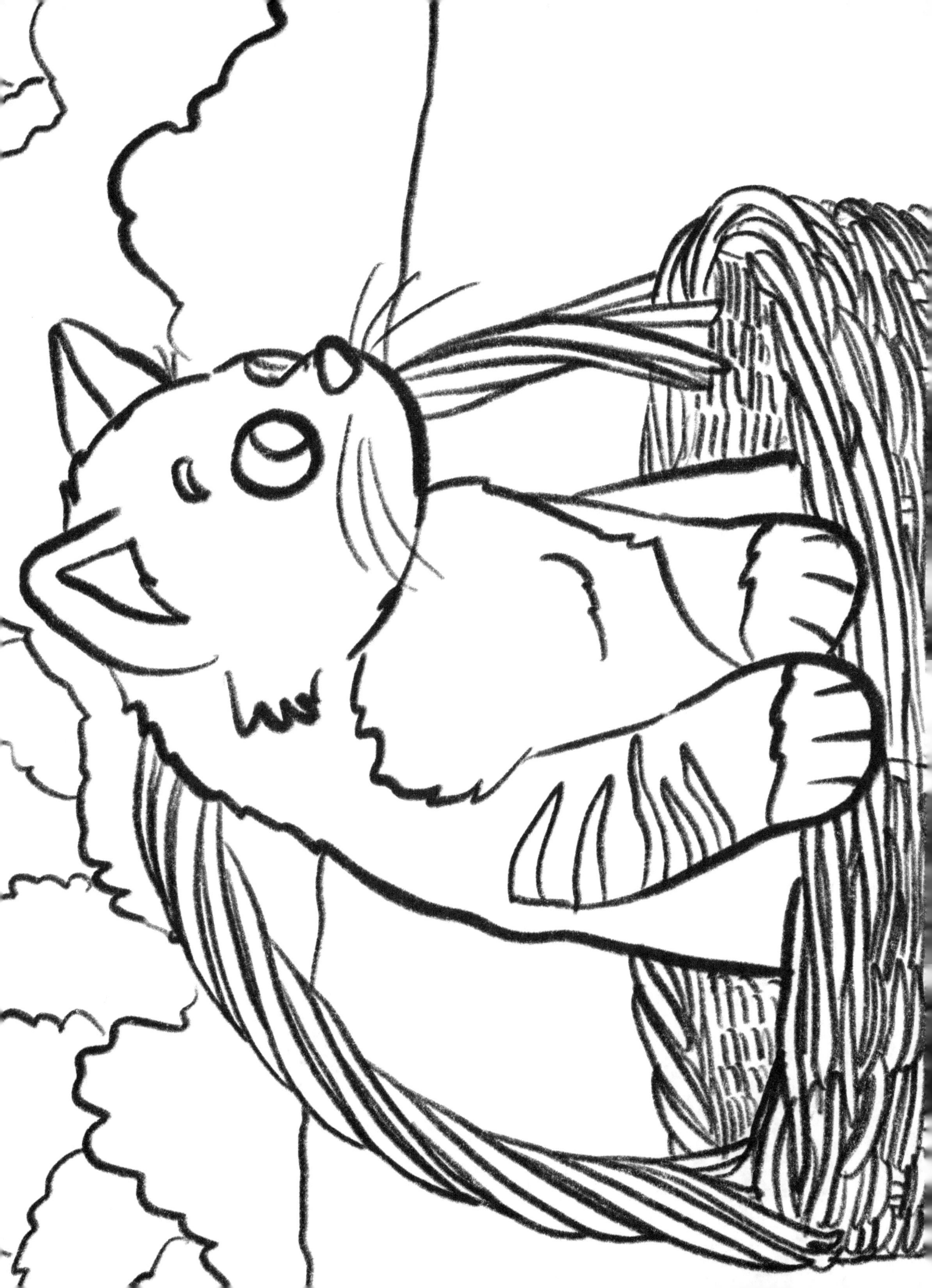

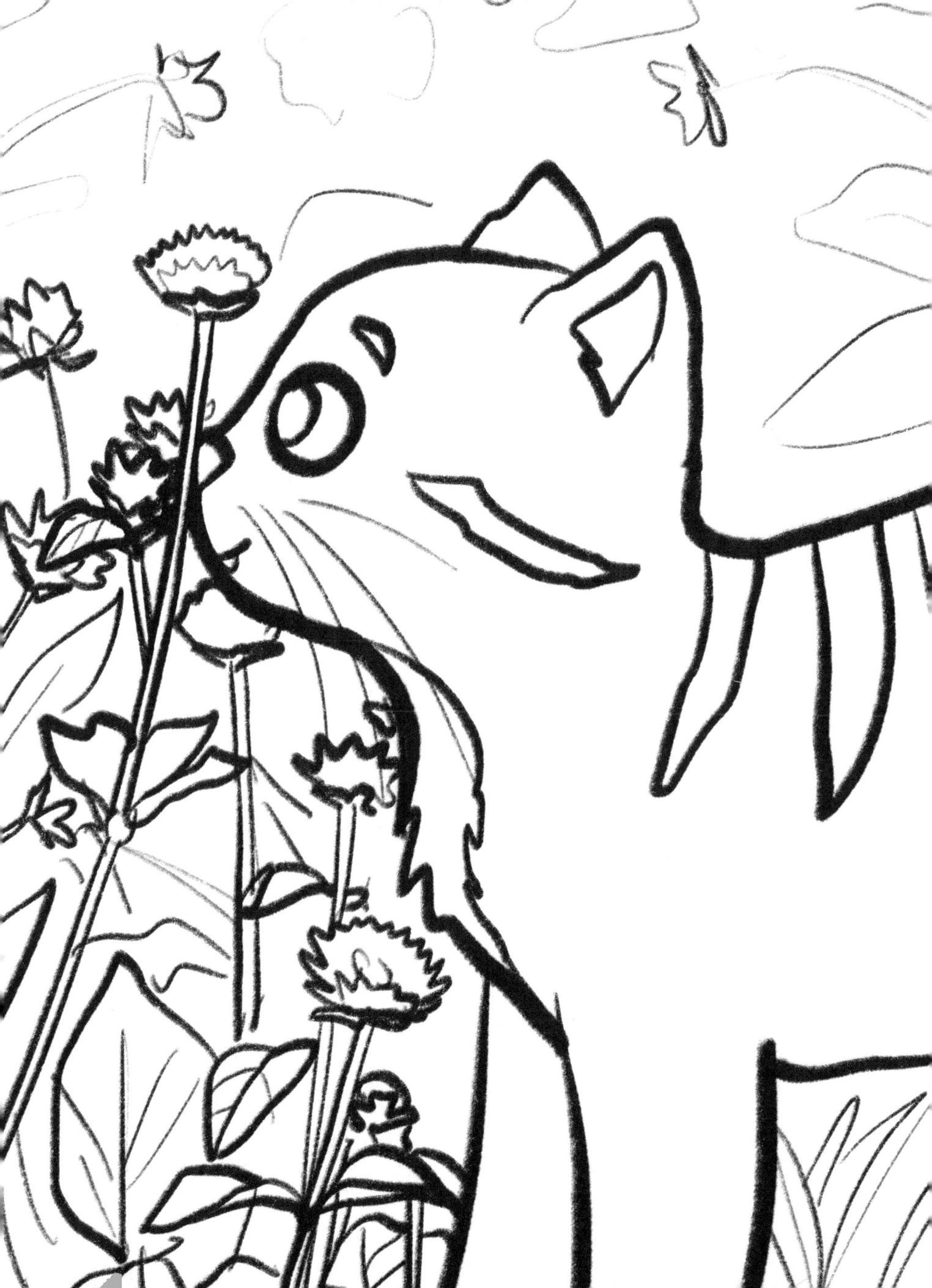

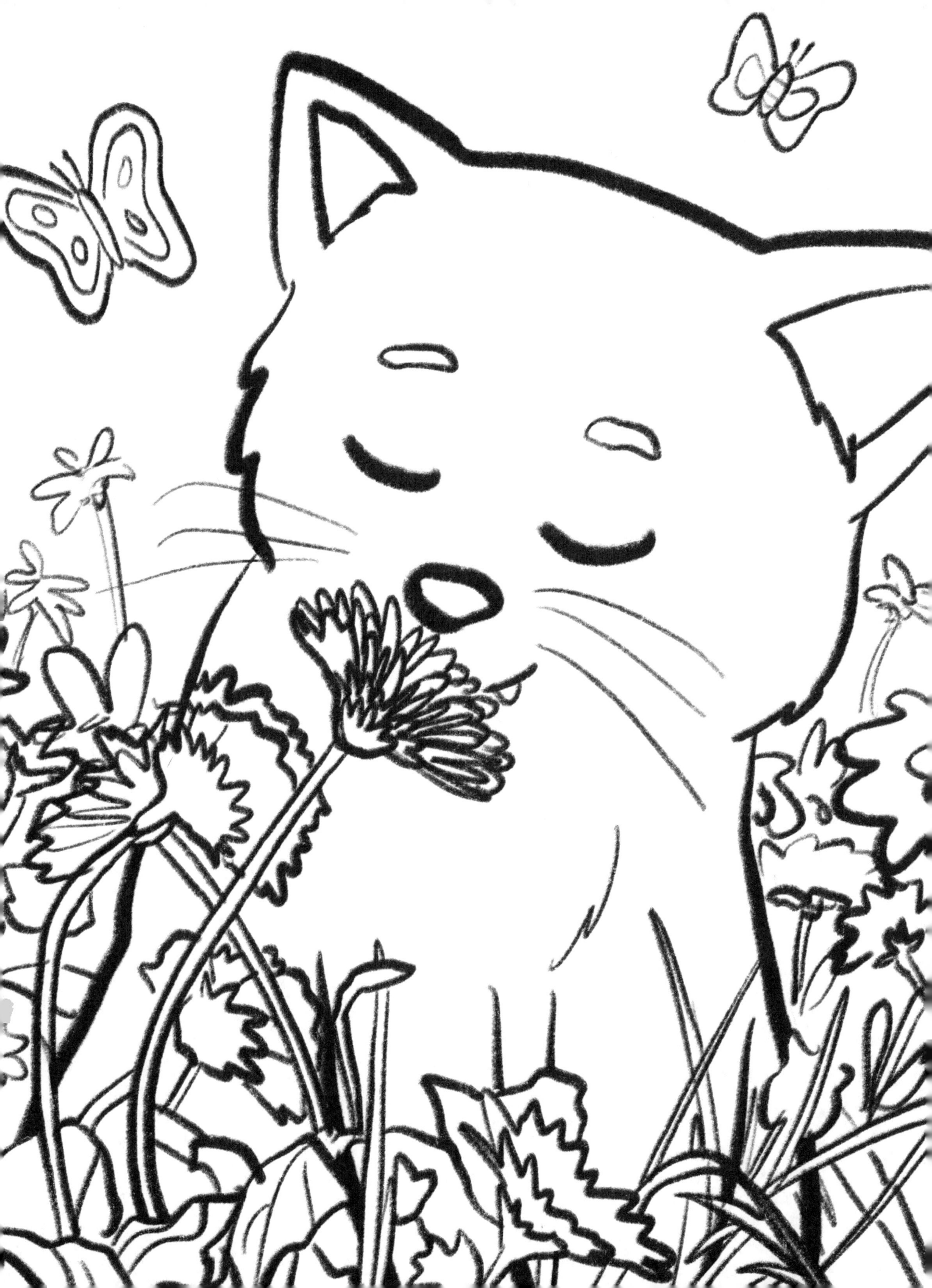

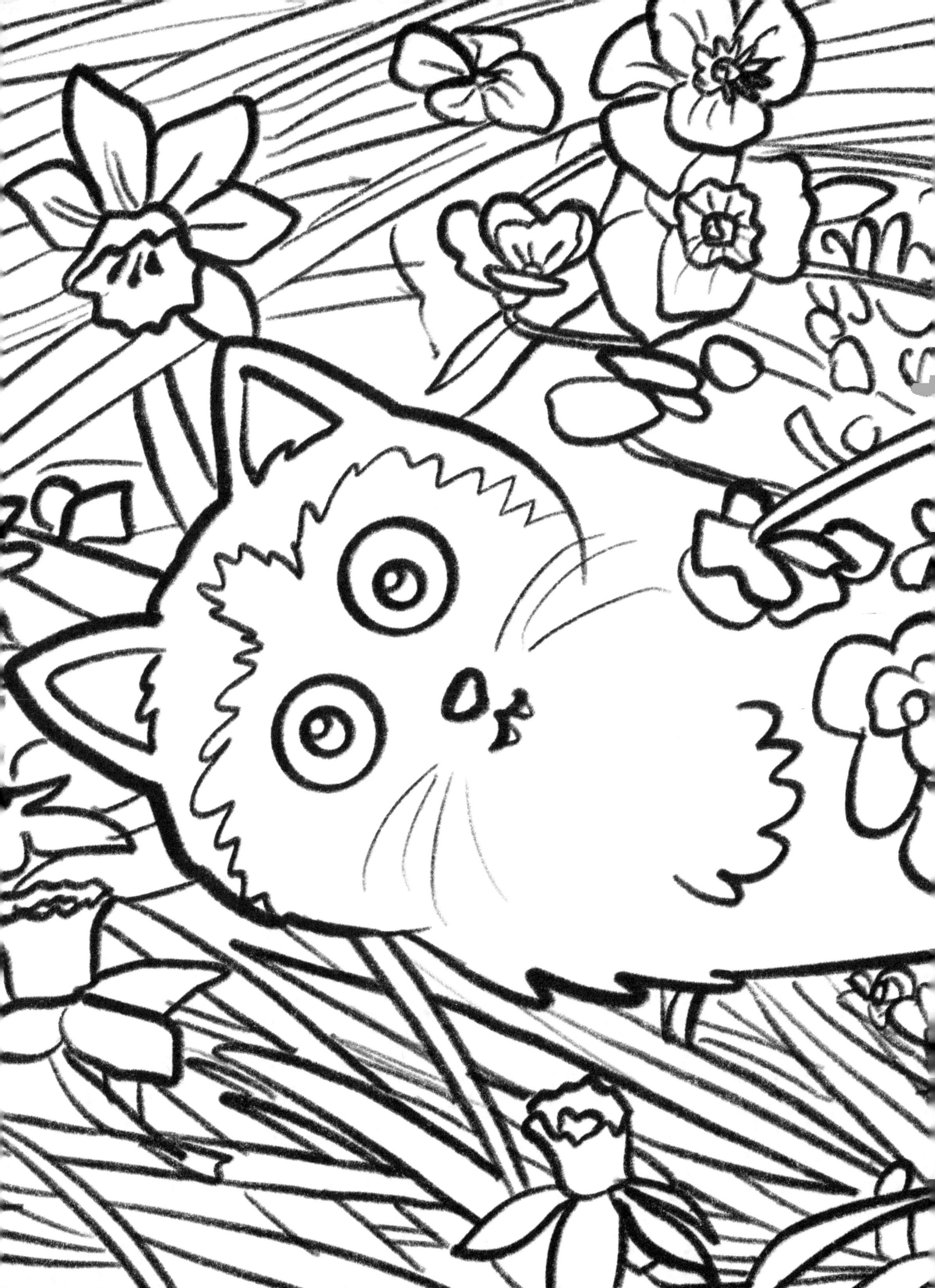

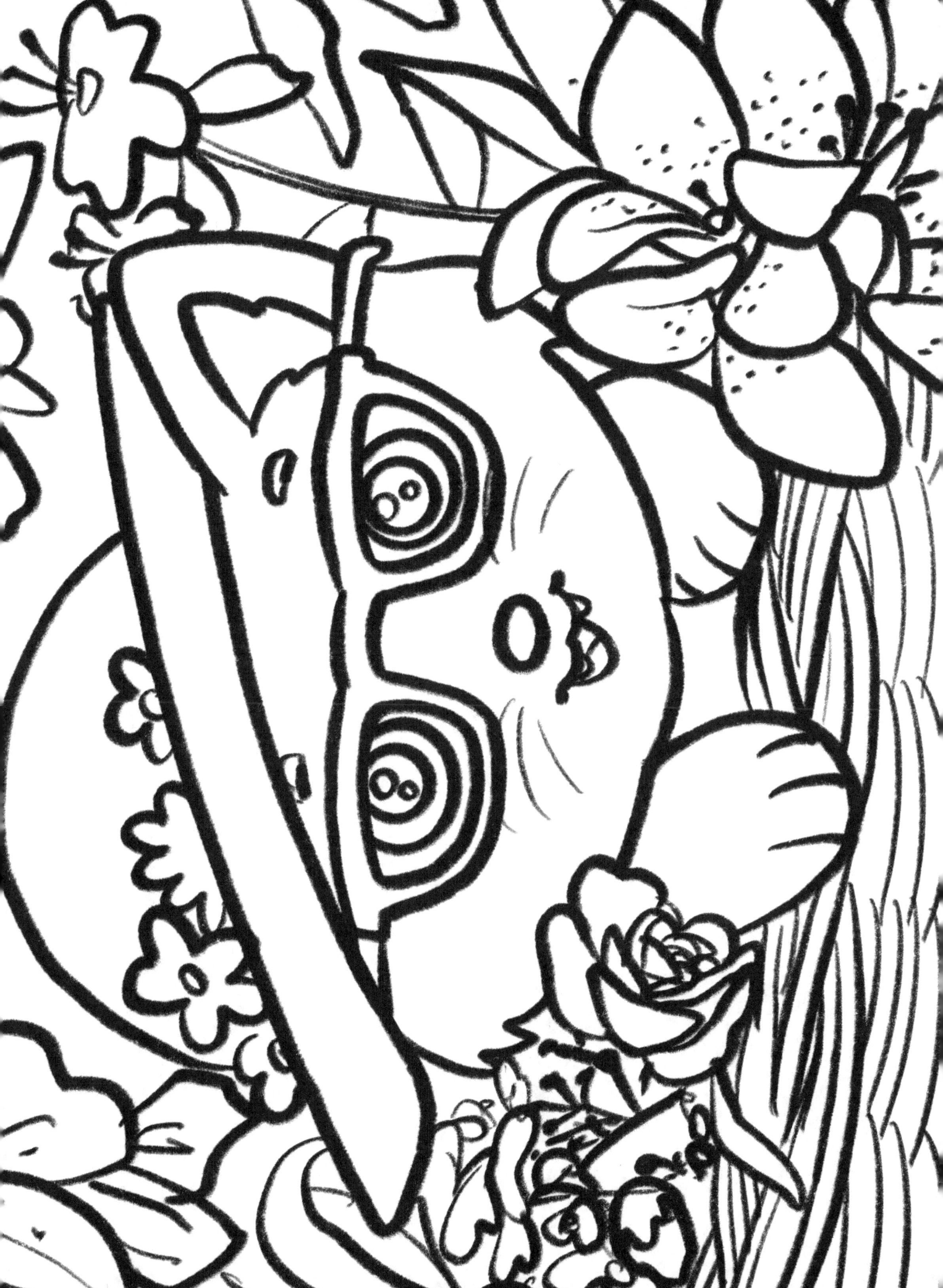

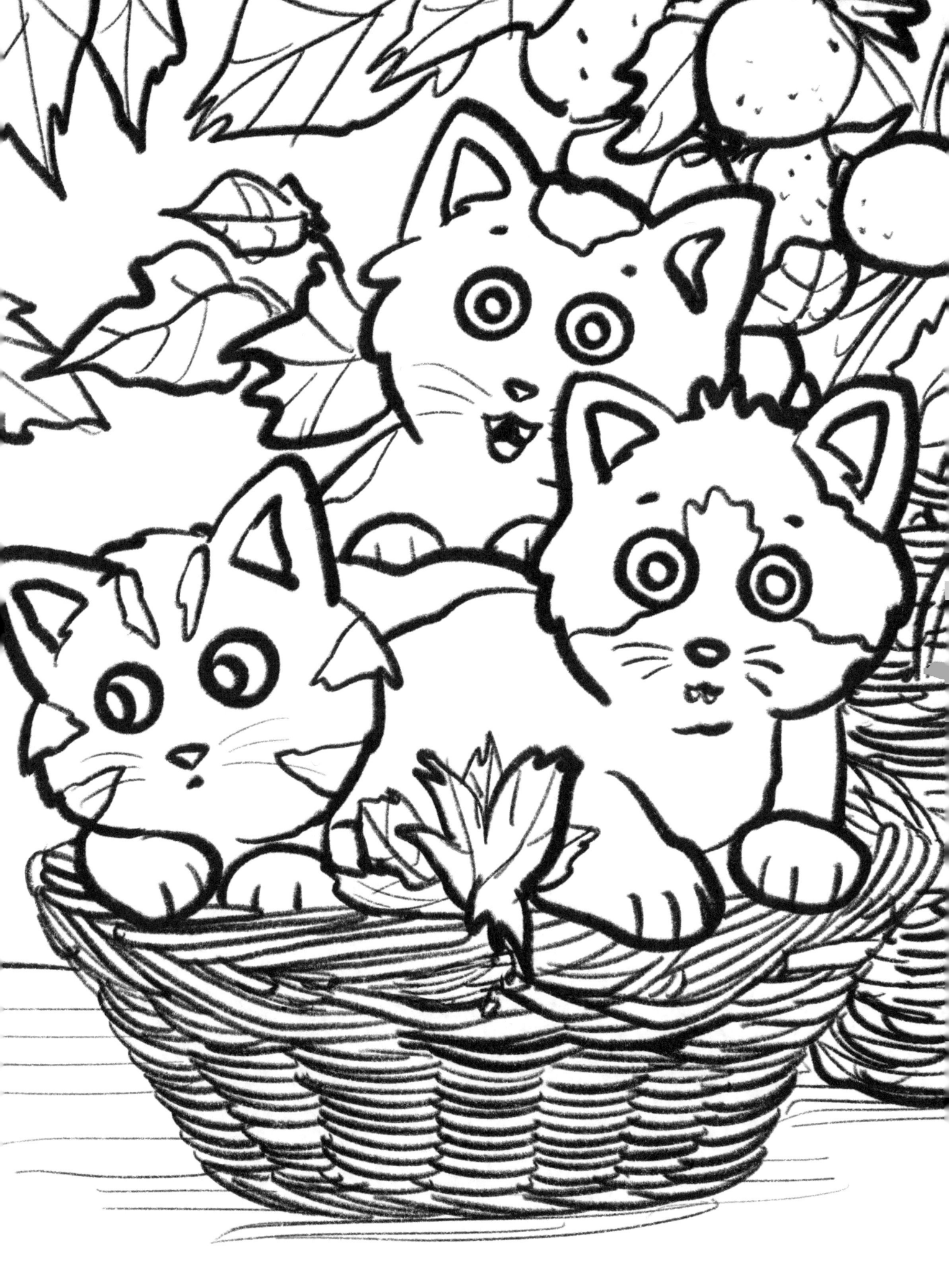

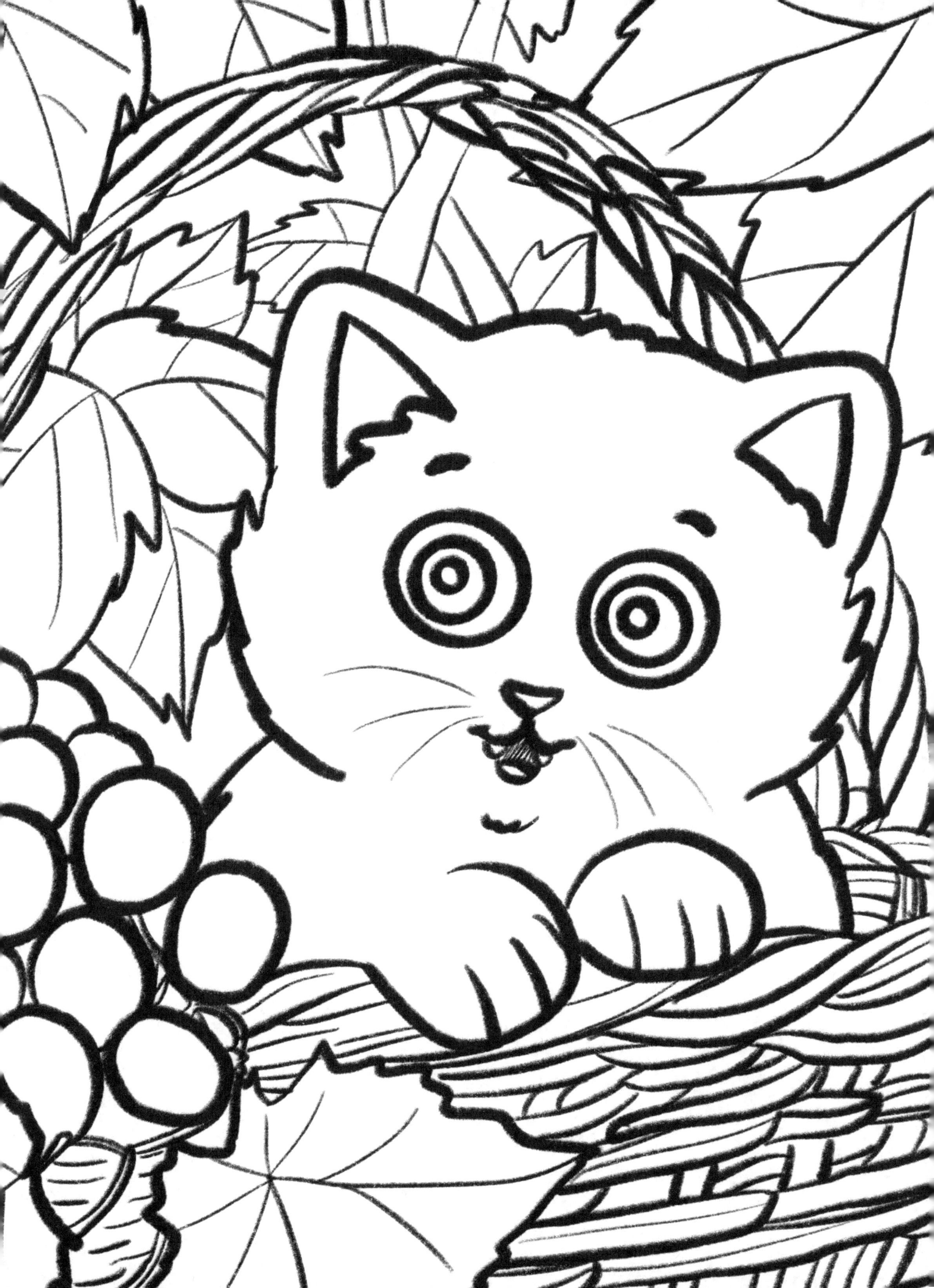

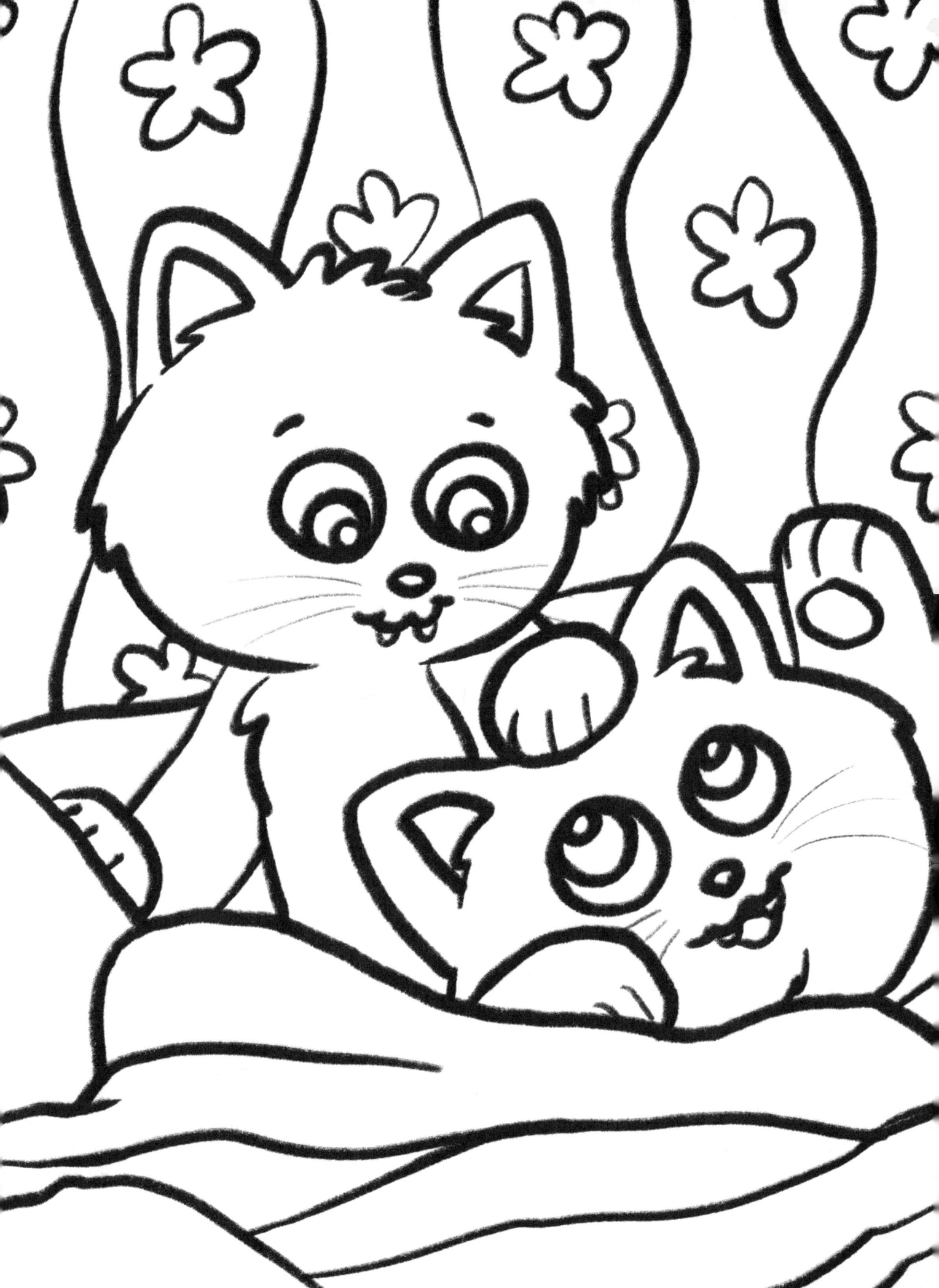

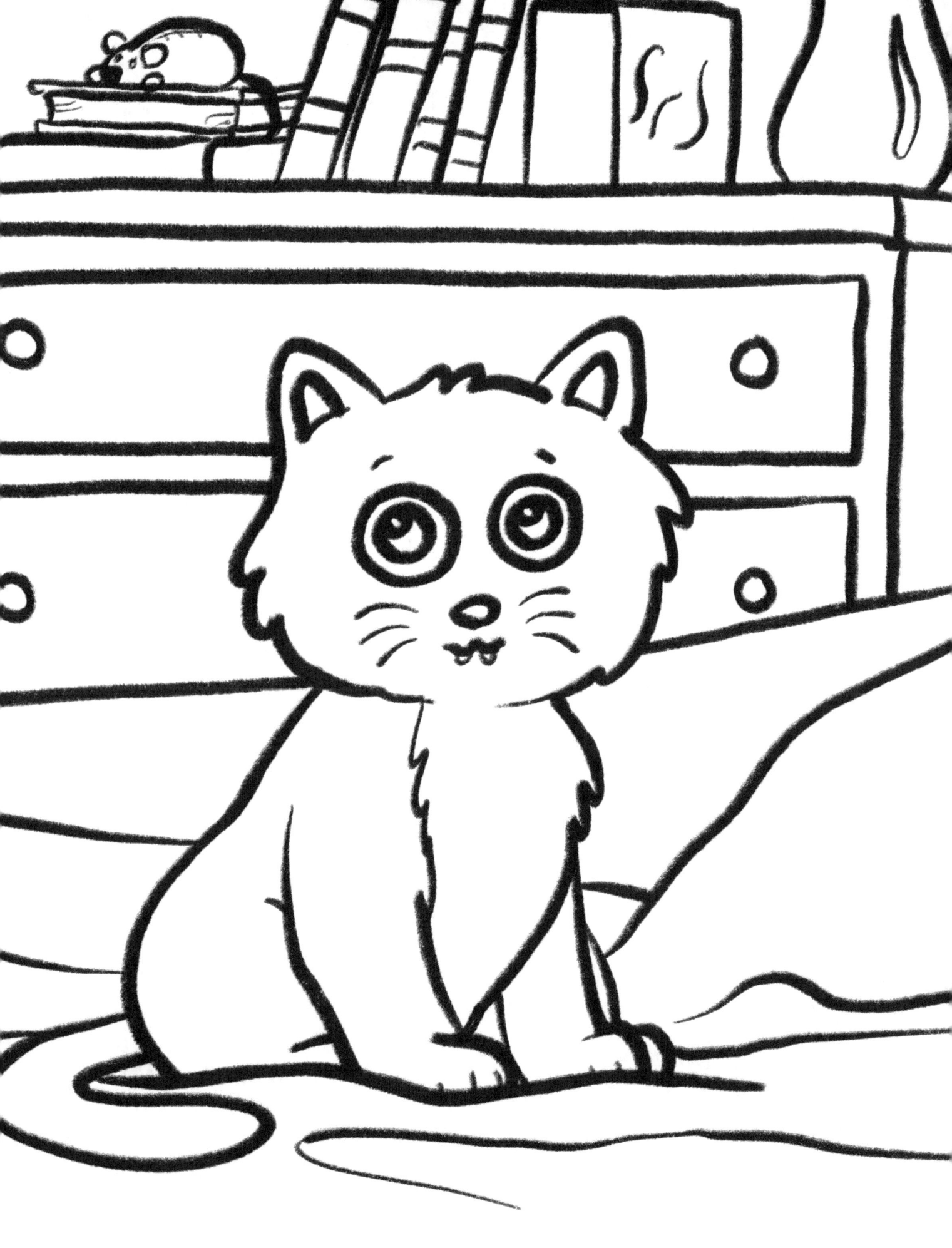

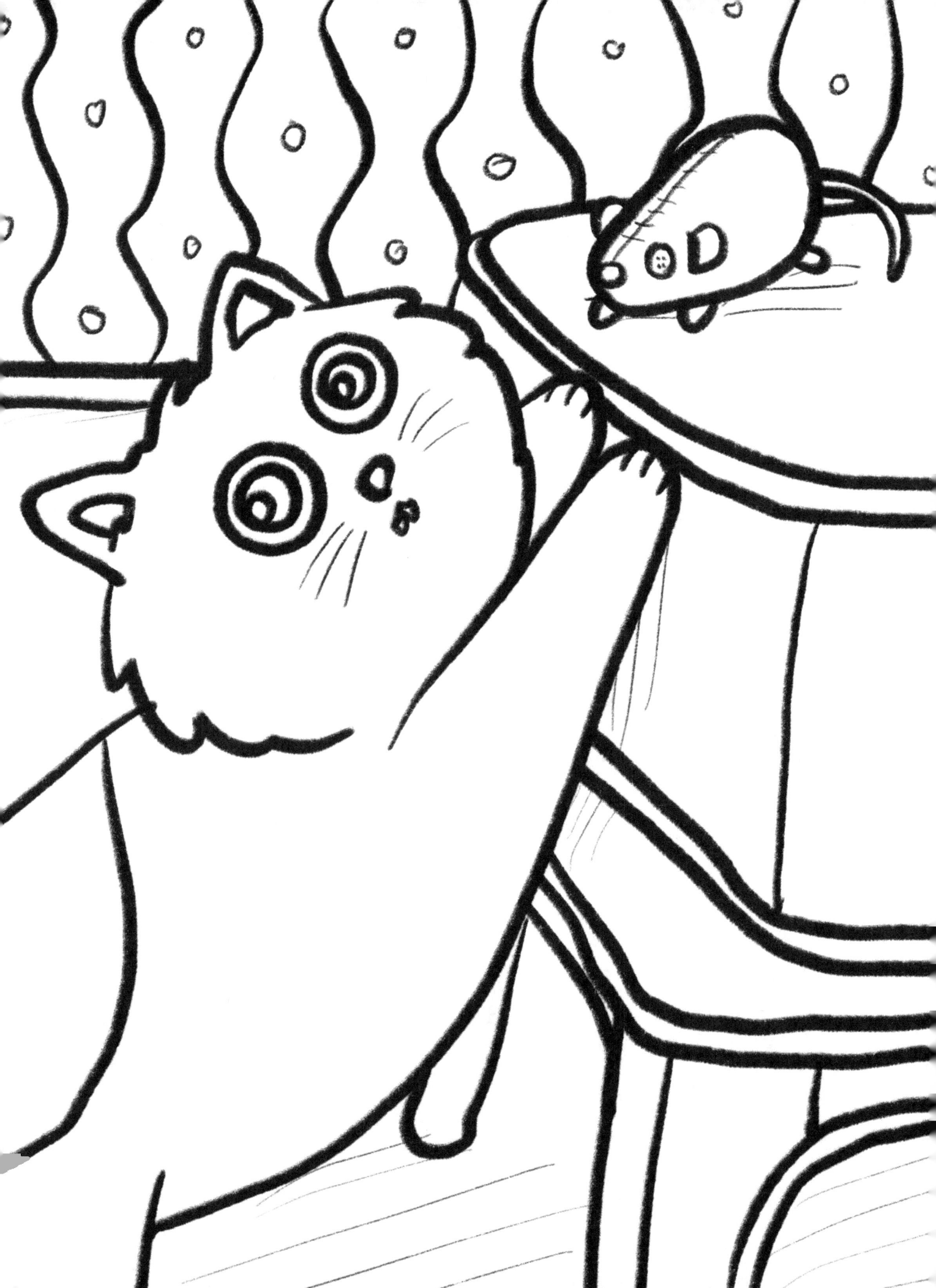

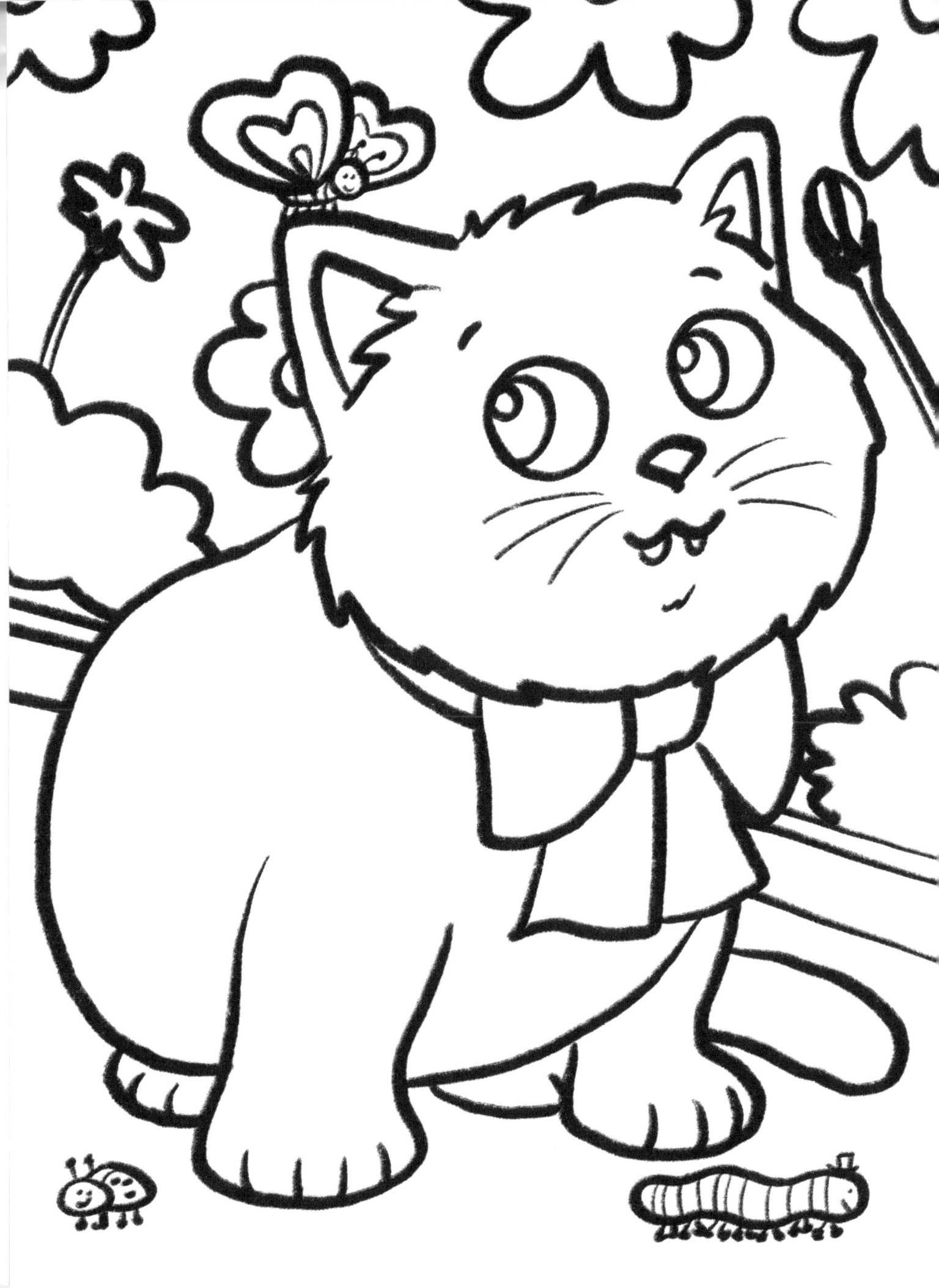

www.ingramcontent.com/pod-product-compliance
Lightning Source LLC
Chambersburg PA
CBHW062233220526
45471CB00009B/3465